The Human Factor

The Human Factor

How Finding Your Dream Job Starts by Getting to Know Yourself

Brent M. Jones

Published by
Connected Events Matter

The Human Factor: How Finding Your Dream Job Starts by Getting to Know Yourself

Copyright © 2023 Brent M. Jones

Published by Connected Events Matter

Copyright © 2023 Connected Events Matter

https://connectedeventsmatter.com/

Contents

Introduction

Despite our many differences, all human beings share at least one thing in common. We all want to be the best version of ourselves.

Some of us define that goal as connecting to a community, having a big family or excelling at a job we love. Others can't necessarily define it, but are seeking that abstract idea of "happiness." Surely, once we find our "purpose" and fulfill it, we will find that elusive "happiness," right?

Alexander Pope said, "Act well your part; there all the honor lies." But what if you find yourself unsure of your place in this world? What if you know your part but find your goals too insurmountable to reach?

You need a change, and in order to get that, you need to change.

Only then will you have the confidence and focus to make that big career change, or learn that new skill to help you jump into another profession. These big life changes can be scary. At times it can seem impossible, especially after feeling as if you've lived a whole life without changing.

Can Human Beings Really Change Though?

Your reading this right now is proof that humans can, and do change.

You have demonstrated the most fundamental evidence of personal development – the willingness to learn. To learn is to first have the desire to improve and grow, which in this case, comes in the form of a self-help book.

Unfortunately for many, reading self-help books isn't an option due to stigmatization – they're skeptical that the books offer any real solutions and are looked down upon by the public. This conclusion is due to a mistaken implication that readers of self-help books are broken and in need of fixing.

The opposite is true. There is a distinction between broken people and those looking to improve. Broken people focus on their negative traits rather than how their good qualities can lift them up. These insecurities stop them from venturing out into the world and discovering new things and ideas due to fear and insecurity.

However, you may think reading a self-help book feels too small to enact any real change. Perhaps that's true, but even the simplest acts are a positive step that leads to another along the lifelong road of personal development.

By reading this, you are already demonstrating the willingness to learn. This book will explore how this trait of yours can lead you to discover some crucial things about yourself and others, giving you the preparation you need to pursue opportunities and your goals, like that elusive, coveted dream job.

First Remember, You Are Human

We aren't broken any more than that we are complete. To begin by acknowledging your journey will never be complete can set you free from feeling too overwhelmed with your perceived place in this world and the road ahead.

It may be tempting to compare yourself to those who have achieved the success you desire, but even this can be counterproductive if it stunts you from even taking those first crucial steps.

Everyone begins from their own place, and the power to strive for more than our lot lies within the choices we make everyday.

This book aims to focus your perspective on how to sustainably continue making those small choices for your own personal development by becoming more self-aware of our identity and talents. This ultimately impacts our capacity to change, gives us the confidence to take action, leading you toward achieving gains never before imagined.

To Change, Tell Yourself a Story. Your Story.

Your Story

In the last twenty-plus years I had the opportunity to tell my own life story in front of a church group of men at least twenty times. At first it was strange saying details about my life out loud as if it were a book, with its own plots, themes, timelines and characters.

Then I found that each subsequent time I shared my story, it became a little different as I added, changed or withheld certain details or events. I had given my life more thought and had new experiences which altered my memory as time passed – I recalled events differently because I would see them in a new light after reflection.

During that same time frame, I heard a few dozen men present their life stories and then heard many tell them again after a few years. The emphasis, substance, and even conclusions of their stories changed for them, as had my own with each new telling.

It turns out life stories are like books in many ways, in which we are simultaneously its protagonist, villain and author. We choose the parts of our lives important to us and connect these events in a narrative, shaping and reshaping our self-identity.

Why Does My Story Matter?

"How you arrange the plot points of your life into narrative shapes says who you are and is a fundamental part of being human," said Monisha Pasupathi, a professor of developmental psychology at the University of Utah in her 2015 article in The Atlantic, "Life's Stories." "In order to have relationships, we've all had to tell little pieces of our story."

Becoming aware of our own stories has utility beyond personal development, and is usable in everyday interactions. We share our life stories in our own small talk: "Hi, where are you from?" "Where did you grow up?"

"Which school did you attend?"

Recently, I watched a salesperson standing at the entrance of a store in a local mall, making eye contact and smiling as people passed by. A lady greeted the salesperson back, and the two of them walked into the store together. I overheard the salesperson asking the customer where she was from. She mentioned a town in California where she grew up, and the salesperson replied with enthusiasm, as she knew the town well. They reminisced about a street they shared in common. Both women relaxed and enjoyed getting to know each other. It was clear they had made a connection by sharing part of their life story.

People like these come and go in our lives, some becoming significant characters in our story as events unfold, but then later in life seem less important. We look back at these people, filtering all we have been through with our memories. Some feel God sends the people that are needed. Others may bring challenges and darkness.

We have a choice in how we build our life's narrative to determine who we are now, and who we will become. We can embrace the events that have impacted us, dissect why they were so important, then weave and reweave them into our story. Choosing to keep perspective can make all the difference as we face new obstacles and forks down the road.

Some believe that people don't change, that we

are wired a certain way until the day we die. This deterministic view of our identity posits that since we didn't choose the time or place where we were born, we are therefore programmed by cause and effect, resulting in our current circumstances.

However, you will find that if you tell your story to a friend or family member, or write it down for yourself, then check back in with your story later, you will find your story to be different.

This is proof that your story, that you use to connect with others, is your identity, and it changes.

Why Other Stories Matter Too

"'A reader lives a thousand lives before he dies,' said Jojen. 'The man who never reads lives only one.'" ⊠ George R.R. Martin, "A Dance with Dragons."

You thought about how your personal story made you who are you today. But you don't live on an island. To learn what makes you human necessitates more than looking inward. You must also be curious to find other points of view. Other perspectives shine light on our own lives.

Art, music, poetry, literature, service to others and even food can influence us to the point where they can become part of our life story. Since humans are social animals, our lives are actually made up of several influences that construct the way we see the world. It informs us how we view our surroundings and our various roles within our family, friends and community.

Author Tony Hillerman wrote about the Navajo people, "Everything is connected. The wing of the corn beetle affects the direction of the wind, the way the sand drifts, the way the light reflects into the eye of man beholding his reality. All is part of totality, and in this totality, man finds his Hozro, his way of walking in harmony, with beauty all around him."

We can expand our own experience by finding more about the human experiences of others – their struggles, lessons, emotional responses and aspirations.

Authors are the gatekeepers to the lives they explore. Harold Bloom, a well-known professor of literature at Yale, has written many books about interesting authors. His book "Shakespeare, The Invention of the Human" claims that the playwright's vocabulary of 22,000 words made him well equipped to express the diverse experience of humankind. Therefore, according to Bloom, Shakespeare "invented the human," or at least a more complete definition of humanness as communicated through written storytelling.

In an interview published in 1995, Bloom reflected on the great authors of the Western world, stating the importance of reading and studying Shakespeare, Dante, Chaucer and Cervantes. He said of these authors that "They provide an intellectual, I dare say, a spiritual value which has nothing to do with organized religion or the history of institutional belief... They tell us things we couldn't possibly know without them, and they reform our minds. They make us more vital." Indeed, Bloom defines humanness using the stories and writings of authors, rather than his own life story, which proves how much the authors Bloom studied are a part of him.

Shakespeare's quotes seem to reflect a deep understanding of humanness that resonate with our lives today. For example:

- *"There is nothing good or bad, only thinking makes it so." —Hamlet*

- *"Hell is empty, and the devils are here." —The Tempest*

- *"Though this be madness, yet there is method in it." —Hamlet*

- *"All that glistens is not gold." —The Merchant of Venice*

- *"To thine own self be true, and it must follow, as the night the day, thou canst not then be false to any man." —Hamlet*

The meaning of life is much more than our own personal daily experiences, and by reading, we can learn from others' experiences without having to also endure them. For example, Hyeonseo Lee's "The Girl with Seven Names: Escape from North Korea" gave me perspective of what it's like living under a totalitarian regime without having to suffer the personal experience myself. By embracing nonfiction accounts of others, you too can be a witness to many different kinds of lives.

Even fiction brings us insight into our humanness. The suspense and twisting plots of fiction writer Lee Child in his "Jack Reacher" series takes us places we would never go and into situations we would never find ourselves. We find excitement, empathy and emotional experience in fiction.

Poetry can also challenge the status quo in our lives and, by doing so, improve the human condition of all people. The work of Maya Angelou, for example, exposes the plights and triumphs of a marginalized people, fighting for equality and justice.

By reading, the knowledge learned through hearing others' stories gives meaning to our own lives, and inspires us for reach for something more.

Why Inspiration Is So Important

You look inward to tell your own story and outward to learn from others. At times, you may have felt inspired, or influenced mentally and emotionally to do something creative. But what is the purpose of being inspired?

Inspiration is energy that channels you toward a goal, pulling you along and motivating you. Without some inspiration, it is harder to act on what you want.

A highly motivated person takes an idea into the real world and won't let anybody interfere with them. That's the person who isn't going to stop as obstacles inevitably arise. They keep going.

By living your life open minded to other perspectives and our shared humanity, you can then be equipped to adapt once pitfalls stand in your path.

However, motivation alone can't help you along life's journey. It's the inspiration working in tandem with motivation that grounds you in the real world.

Other Ways to Find That Coveted Inspiration

This list of 17 sources for inspiration concludes with, "You are the source for your inspiration." This acknowledges that only you and your individual perception can feel inspiration. You own it.

How you feel when you listen to music will not be created by the music but how the music influences you. You recreate yourself as your inspiration finds new ways to see your own experiences.

- Listen to music

- Dance

- Close your eyes

- Read books
- Pick a subject to research
- Go for a walk
- Climb a mountain
- Walk amongst trees
- Listen the wind blow through the leaves
- Meditate and listen to silence.
- Listen to your audience
- Spend time with your family and friends
- Go to a favorite place
- Spend time looking at art
- Daydream
- Engage with mentors and teachers
- You are the source for your inspiration

How to Channel
This Inspiration Into
Building Your Career

"Burnout" in a career is a very real thing.

"The Great Resignation" revealed how an astounding portion of the labor force quit or wants to resign from their jobs to try something else. The reported reasons for this include boredom at work, anxiety, fatigue, depression, frustration, difficulty concentrating, lack of creativity and loss of trust.

I was talking with an old friend about his successful career and he told me that he felt his longevity in his industry was seen as a negative, not a positive by some in his field and he had begun to think it was true. How could this be? Himself and others should view his vast experience as "added wisdom" gained by trial and error. His viewpoint spoke loudly to his own burnout, but is this what years of work can lead to?

The dictionary definition of burnout is "the end of the powered stage in a rocket's flight when the propellant has been used up." With people, a lot of energy perusing various goals is spent, and when people are burned out, they feel somewhat used up and complacent.

You can hear the burnout in someone saying, "We tried that once before and it didn't work so it won't work now." My friend worked in the food service industry and like many industries it is dynamic – customer's preferences change. That should present challenges and opportunities to force us to rethink what we "always knew."

As a business executive and career development coach with decades of experience, I advised my friend to become a student of his industry. Think of new approaches or new ways to use old products and concepts. This will provide you renewed energy. As a veteran you shouldn't worry about making a mistake. I told him that he of all people should know that a failure or setback is actually an opportunity. When any of us start worrying about burnout, we should stop thinking about the past and look toward the future.

As business analyst and author Peter Drucker, has said, "The best way to predict the future is to create it."

It's time to put your combined motivation and inspiration to use. To successfully walk the path toward the future you want, you first need to take stock of where you are in the present. Otherwise, you may take a wrong turn and have to start over.

Having looked inward at your own story, and became inspired by others' stories, devote this accumulated energy toward figuring out what's most important to you in life – your unique purpose.

Figuring Out Your Purpose

Mark Twain said, "The two most important days in your life is the day you were born and the day you find out why."

Why are we here? You may have asked yourself this once or twice. Is our life's purpose to be happy? Perhaps, and there's some logic to it.

Newborns seek happiness and that is the main purpose in their lives. But as they grow older, they recognize that others provide the things that lead to happiness. A child loves because he is loved first and feels love from others before understanding it. Higher self-esteem improves academic performance and better parent-child communication. On the other hand, children who do not have affectionate parents tend to have fewer positive outcomes on all these same measures.

The lesson is that those who consistently help others are happy and less likely to be overcome with self-imposed obstacles such as stress. The subsequent experiences they have then result in their own improved mental health.

So, I pose the question again - is our purpose to be happy, or help others? The two actually feed each other. As adults we serve each other in our individual lives and community, resulting in a sustained, meaningful happiness.

It's no coincidence that the most meaningful factor in building a successful career is defined by investing in oneself by serving others – networking.

The Importance of Networking

Maybe you have heard someone going through a frustrating job search say something along these lines: "They got the job because they knew somebody," or "They were hired because of their connections."

One of the biggest challenges job seekers may face is the simple fact that the vast majority of open positions are never posted or publicized. Word spreads and jobs are filled before hiring managers even consider hanging up the "Help Wanted" sign. According to online professional networking site LinkedIn, 80% of job openings are never posted and up to 85% of all jobs are filled by networking.

Even when job openings are posted, often to follow fair hiring practice mandates, it is common for employers to have already decided on a hire before the job is posted.

Why would this many jobs never be listed? One reason is that it seems hiring managers prefer to either hire from within or have candidates referred to them by people they know and trust. Another factor is that word gets out internally before jobs are publicly posted and the insiders pass the information to their own contacts.

Job seeking is even more challenging if you're searching while unemployed. LinkedIn data shows that 70% of the global workforce is made up of so-called passive talent. These are working employees not actively searching but still keeping an eye on job postings and opportunities in case something interests them.

These passive job seekers, which make up about 87 majority of those looking for jobs, can take their time doing research and reach out to their networking contacts. Potential employers, for the same reasons as you, want to find strong candidates whose experience, strengths and skills match up with the job description, so also take their time passively looking. Good companies know that good matches result in motivated, happy employees who help build the company, so it really pays off to take their time with this decision.

Unfortunately, it's generally easier to find a job when you already have one. Employers assume that if a job seeker is already employed, he or she must have the skills, experience, and drive to be employable. Between preferring candidates referred to them and those who are currently employed, active job seekers have to work a lot harder to overcome this. This is why strategic networking is so important.

But where to even begin when it comes to proper networking? Rest assured, the skills and strategies detailed in the following pages serve job seekers long after they land that coveted job, as powerful weapons for long-term success in both career and life, beginning with knowing your own story, intimately and honestly.

Use Your Built-Up Knowledge of Yourself to Find The Job You Really Want

After looking inward and giving serious thought to your own story, you may discover that a major purpose in your life is career-related. You may also find that you haven't achieved your goals yet, or are unhappy in your current employment situation.

If so, you're not alone, and there's something you can do about it. Reports show that the average person changes careers 5-7 times during their working life. With an ever-increasing number of career choices, 30% of the workforce change careers or jobs every 12 months. Employees don't expect their job to last a lifetime anymore and today's employers often don't see their employees as lifelong commitments.

But remember that inspiration needs to work in tandem with motivation, and it will help you find a company that will make you happier, not just as unhappy.

By examining your own story, you can discover exactly why you want to move on and change jobs and/or companies. Take an honest look at your own strengths, abilities and what's important to you. Knowing these things about yourself will help focus your job search and make for a better fit in the new company.

Let's say you find that the ideal job for you requires skills you don't have. Now you have the inspiration to learn those new skills and prepare for this career change.

But how do you know which skills to learn or what steps to take to land that dream job? To make informed decisions it helps to gain insight from an industry insider. But what if you're stepping into another industry where you don't have an existing network? There is a tried-and-true method you can use to build a new network or expand the one you have – the informational interview.

The Informational Interview and Why It's Valuable

Everyone has a network, but many people do not recognize, develop, or nurture it until they find themselves out of work. That is a mistake, but one easily rectified. Informational networking is a great tool to find answers about how to break into an industry, career or job.

The informational interview is networking with a purpose – to create a professional or social contact where information is exchanged. One party communicates about who they are, and the other communicates what the first party wants to learn.

Traditionally, the purpose of this type of interview is doing relevant research by engaging those on the front lines of the targeted subject matter. By speaking directly with an expert in person, on the phone or online, you can likely obtain information you could not otherwise gain through other types of research. You also have an opportunity to hear relevant real-life stories and firsthand accounts, as well as suggestions of other places to look or other people to consult for the information you are seeking.

While gathering information is important, the value of the personal component should not be underestimated. Consider, who are the people whose friendships and relationships you value the most and why do they stand out? At our core, we like to be around people who ask us questions and listen. You can even say our best friends and relationships are experts at conducting informational interviews. They get us to do the talking and we just spill our thoughts out. We then get to know how to help each other out in each other's lives, much like a network.

In addition, all that work you did to clarify your own story and the importance of others' really comes in handy here. By being able to speak honestly about yourself clearly and succinctly, you will more efficiently establish a connection with others.

Some people with some experience in their industry mischaracterize informational interviews as being only appropriate for beginners in their job market. Those same people are at risk of having a narrow view of their own industry and can easily come across as dated or behind the times in an interview. They also may not get the necessary perspective to see how their skills could easily fit in a related industry. Successful people are always students, and these types of interviews are opportunities for anyone to stay relevant.

As a career development coach, I have often been surprised to learn that a job-seeking candidate has reached the interview phase before even understanding the company's business and product. In those cases, they will seem ill prepared compared to the other candidates.

Who to Contact for Informational Interviews and How to Get Started

Eleanor Roosevelt said "Never allow a person to tell you no, who doesn't have the power to say yes." This quote shows an important way to think about networking and illustrates an important principle. If you ask people to hire you or help you in your job search and they can't, you've probably done a poor job of networking. Informational interviews and asking the right questions of your connections will take you to the "right" person – the one who can say yes!

So how do you find these "right" ones who'll say yes? Chances are you already have some to contact for referrals right now. Your job search network consists of everyone you know, from former co-workers and supervisors to company executives, trade association employees, suppliers, online connections, customers and competitors.

An even better network contact than an immediate past co-worker might be someone who left your prior company a while back and went somewhere else. Their past relationship with you and the change they made can make them exceptional resources to learn about opportunities for you. You will want to know their perspective now on the marketplace with their new company. Where do they see your skills fitting best in the current environment? Are there any new skills they advise you to learn to get the best opportunities?

Your previous company's competitors and suppliers can be additional excellent network contacts. A supplier may have called your company as well as its competitors for years. They know who is growing and hiring and who the right contacts may be.

Even customers of your former company can result in an opportunity. Your insights and experience as a former supplier could be an asset to them.

All have different perspectives of the industry and marketplace and can suggest ideas and approaches that you will likely miss. Both the suppliers and customers will have different viewpoints of your companies' competitors. You will want to find out who really are the leaders in your category and what they're doing differently.

Professional contacts aside, helpful members of our network can also be our friends, neighbors or even members of your church congregation. Some of those contacts may coincidentally be connected or know someone relevant in an industry or company you're researching. All you're looking for at first is a name to call and the name of who referred you.

If you're at church, a PTA meeting or family gathering it can be surprising how easy it is to just ask: Does anyone know anyone who works in the aerospace industry, or is a retail manager (or in whatever field you seek)? By putting yourself out there enough, you will find someone who does.

The next step is to let them know you're looking to learn more about that industry and hope to get a 30-minute interview to pick the brain of an expert. Ask if you can call or email their contact and use their name to explain why you reached out to meet and ask questions. If your contact knows you were referred then more time may be made available to you. Ask if they'll agree to speak with you briefly to share their insights when it's convenient for them.

The same process applies to contacts you make

online. LinkedIn is the largest professional network in the world and has in many ways replaced many traditional networking approaches. It also has created shortcuts and the process of opening doors for informational interviews.

Using LinkedIn makes it easy to research companies of interest, their staff of employees, some of whom you may already know. You only need to click "connect" and perhaps include a note, but too often with people you don't know this is where the connection ends. While LinkedIn has provided a way to find these connections, virtual interactions don't measure up to having a real history. Still, LinkedIn makes it easy to seek out company information and is a wonderful tool in a number of ways.

What You Want to Learn When Informational Networking

A job for most of us is more than just a way to make a living. It shapes how we see ourselves, as well as how others see us. It gives our days structure, purpose and meaning. With such an important decision to make when we seek new employment, it's obvious that we need to be well prepared when picking a company to potentially join. We want to know if we really do fit a job description, the company's culture and if we have the right knowledge about the industry.

The three key areas to research in order to be fully

prepared for that big interview are this job's industry, the company and the job itself.

An industry is a group of companies that are related based on their primary business activities. For example, retail grocery is an industry, consisting of many kinds of in-store jobs, and also the store suppliers and distributors. Each of those sectors has their own variety of jobs, as do the manufacturers that service those distributors and stores. Depending on the role you seek, the industry could be considered one big industry or just a segment of it.

Learning about the industry first will give you credibility when you meet with people from these companies and then take that knowledge when interviewing for the job.

One area to learn is the language of that particular industry, sometimes known as trade jargon. When exposed to this you will want to make notes and remember since potential employers would feel confident you could hit the ground running with suppliers.

An example of this would be in the restaurant supply industry. From both the manufacturer and distributor point of view, the ultimate customer of their product is the "end-user." For the restaurant this will not mean much but it is quite common terminology in the supply chain. Understanding where to use the word "supply chain" is another good example.

An informational interview offers you a number of

opportunities to learn, such as if your prior perceptions of the industry are accurate. You can also learn about the companies and their competition. If you are working in the industry already, your suppliers can tell you which competitors are doing well. They are supplying them with many of the same things your past company used, and they know who is growing and who is not. These suppliers will be careful with confidential information, but they will want to help you find a place and will be glad if you become a customer.

Meeting with someone in the industry or a past supplier can point you toward the good companies and the next place to seek an informational interview. A former co-worker now employed at a competitor can be especially helpful in referring you to speak with someone at their company. You will benefit by learning about a particular company before you apply there.

Overall, if you are applying for a specific job, it seems obvious that knowing as much as you can about that job will help you. Seek others in the industry who have the same job and ask them for an informational interview. Their advice and comments may be the best preparation you can get for your job interview. Pay attention to the way they refer to the different parts of their work. Their everyday keywords and job lingo will make you sound and seem like a good fit.

The Interview

Interviews can be conducted in person, over the phone, or via video conferencing. However, the value of connecting with someone increases drastically if that interaction is face-to-face, or at least on Zoom or Google Meet.

Having an in-person conversation builds rapport more than any email could achieve. Having this time together builds a foundation of trust that could lead the interviewed to share information they wouldn't otherwise provide. Just by merely looking each other in the eye can sometimes convey more than mere words could.

When the interview is finished, ask if you can follow up after you do some additional research based on what you learned from the meeting. Your goal is to learn about three areas: the industry, the company, and the job. If you can show that you understand the company, its structure and organization in this first meeting or when you return, you will come across as sincere in your interest and will likely be given more help, maybe even other referrals.

Remember however that this is an informational interview only, so do not ask for a job. Your objective is to learn and find out where you need to go to learn more. Be sure to thank the contact for the time and follow up with a written email note. Also, your contacts throughout the searching process all merit follow up thank you notes. For some contacts you'll want to find ways to become a valuable source to them over the coming years.

This approach will take time to really teach you what you need to know, but it will help you better understand an industry as well as companies and jobs within it. It's that depth of understanding that can help you determine what it is that you really want to do.

Asking the Right Questions

You have identified an industry leader or a person who will be able to see the industry more completely than you have so far. You asked for a short appointment, and you have been honest about why you called them. Perhaps a friend recommended them as very successful or knowledgeable, or maybe you have awareness of their role in the industry.

You know you have perhaps 30 minutes to ask questions that will help you in your job and career search exploration. You ask if it is agreeable to take notes and you're careful to not spend too much time talking about yourself, using your "me in 30 seconds speech" (a rehearsed presentation of who you are). You don't want to ask things that would have been easily learned on your own. What is useful is asking the person about their journey to their current position, a description of their day-to-day responsibilities and tips they would offer someone interested in working in their field.

When the interview is over you can review your notes and put into an outline overview of what was discussed and what you learned.

After all that effort, none of this meeting would have been particularly useful without asking the right questions, so preparation is key. Once you get an appointment scheduled, study and read up on the industry and the contact's company so your questions will make sense. A thoughtful, relevant question might result in the contact bringing in or suggesting another person for you to see, even further expanding your network.

To help, here are some occupation-focused questions that you can ask about the person's job or the job you are considering:

1. What is the title of the person you are interviewing? Is this person's title similar to others in the industry with similar jobs? Is the title you're seeking consistent throughout the industry or does it have different titles?

2. What are the duties and skills used during a typical day, week, month, and year? Does the routine of the job change on a day-to-day basis?

3. What educational degrees or certificates are recommended? Which courses are most valuable to gain the skills necessary for success in this occupation?

4. What kind of past work or internship experience would employers look for in a job applicant?

5. What are the important keywords or buzzwords to include in a resume, cover letter or interview dialogue when job searching in the field?

6. What would the advisor suggest as an effective job search approach?

7. What are the main or most important personal characteristics for success in the field?

8. What other departments or kinds of workers frequently interact with this position?

9. Is there evidence of differential treatment between male and female workers with respect to job duties, pay and opportunities for advancement?

10. What are the employment prospects in the advisor's geographic area? Where are the best employment prospects?

11. What are some related occupations?

12. What are the different salary ranges?

13. Does the typical worker have a set schedule, or are the hours flexible?

14. What are the demands and frustrations that typically accompany this type of work?

15. How can you determine that you have the ability or potential to be successful in this specific occupation?

16. Is this a rapidly growing field?

17. What types of technology are used and how are they used?

18. Where are job listings found?

19. What does this industry and companies consider being entry-level positions?

20. What does the advisor know now that would have been helpful to know when she or he was in your shoes?

General Questions to Ask:

21. How many hours do they work?

22. What education does the advisor have?

23. What was the advisor's career path from college to present?

24. What are the satisfying aspects of the advisor's work?

25. What are the greatest pressures, frustrations, or anxieties in the work?

26. What are the major job responsibilities?

27. What are the advisor's toughest problems and decisions?

28. How would the advisor describe the atmosphere/culture of the workplace?

29. Does the advisor think you left out any important questions that would be helpful to learn more about the job or occupation?

30. Can the advisor suggest others who may be valuable sources for you? If you call them, can you use the advisor's name? (This works best at the end of the interview)

31. Express gratitude for the help and also follow up with a thank you note.

How to Use The Information You Learned to Get a Job

Informational interviews do sometimes lead you to job openings. However, your primary goal is to gain insight and knowledge that will enable you to prepare your resume and plan your active job search more strategically. The more you learn about the industry and the companies and jobs within it before you are in consideration for a job, the better you will come across.

Asking your best network contacts about job options follows your informational interview research. In this case, former co-workers and supervisors are excellent contacts because they know you, your previous position, how you fit in the workforce, and your hard and soft skills. If they do pass on information about a job opening, you can and should still go back to the informational interview. Ask for a short meeting with someone at the company before applying so you will be more knowledgeable when trying to get a job interview opportunity.

It's worth noting that potential employers often see a candidate that is currently employed as a stronger potential employee, still valued by his past employer, not someone who was pushed out and considered weaker. Unemployed candidates can easily seem too eager in trying to sell their experience and skills, even in some cases when they aren't the best matches. Passion and excitement displayed for the new job can be misinterpreted as just needing a job rather than a genuine belief that a real contribution can be made. As unfair as this is, being in a position where you don't have to take an offer is an advantage.

Employers will normally reach out to someone with the best job skills, experience and knowledge, so be sure your resume shows skills and strengths that match those requested on the job listing.

Informational Interviews in Summary

When you apply for a job, you should already be prepared for the interview. Yes, knowing yourself and your story is important, but when the time comes, don't walk in without having done the proper research. What you need to know is found by conducting your own informational interviews, a kind of investigative research. Those interviews should take place with people in the same industry, the company where you will be applying and with people who have similar jobs with other companies.

Consider the suppliers, competitors and customers in your target industry. Each of those has a unique perspective on the company and maybe even the job for which you're applying.

The more you know, the better your chances of getting the job and the more valuable you will be perceived in your job interviews. Employers want qualified candidates and if you don't know anything about the industry, company or job, how can you expect to be considered qualified? These types of interviews and personal research help you become qualified before you meet with the employer.

Each person you talk with becomes an ongoing member of your own network and you need to look for opportunities to be of value to them if possible. You can find these contacts by asking your own network. You may not know someone who works in your target areas. However, someone in your existing network might and that will enable you to call for a short meeting and use your mutual network contact to show credibility.

It is important that you treat an information interview request appropriately. Ask only for a short time to ask some questions and learn a little about the person's job and duties. Don't take longer than requested or ask for a job during this time because you told your new contact you just wanted to ask questions.

If no one in your own network can point you toward someone working in the area you target, then ask if they know someone who might. You can call without a name reference but do your best to find a connection. This approach is research focused and will help you understand the industry and become exposed to the language and keywords of the industry.

If you set up and attend several informational interviews before you apply for a job you will find that the job interview will be easier and lead to more success.

Remember, Networking Is Not Just About You

Throughout your career, not just when you're out of work, establish and build your network. Be active with give and take, offering ideas and support to others. Connect with contacts who have the jobs you would like and study them. What paths have their careers taken? LinkedIn will show their work histories: do a little research and see the payoff.

But in order for networking to truly work in the long-term, it needs to be a two-way street. Find ways to help members of your network when you can. Always strive to be a valuable contact yourself and pay it forward. Keep in touch and occasionally offer suggestions and ideas to your contacts. For example, when out in the marketplace interviewing for jobs and spending time on informational interviews, you often will find out things that may not be of value to you but that could be useful to someone in your network. Keep proprietary and confidential information to yourself of course, but share other things that could help or be of interest to your contacts. They'll appreciate it and may one day return the favor.

Remember, to be happy you need to help others, who will in turn help you. Just as in life, a successful career is not achieved in a vacuum.

Use the network you have even if it isn't large and full of professionals to find those that can provide an informational interview. This will expand your network and you can begin to have different subgroups in your network. Work to be of value to those in your network so that you can get value from them.

Informational interviews are essential if you want to break into a new industry and even if you're familiar with jobs and companies the approach has various benefits.

Your efforts will give you visibility and exposure as well as an environment that is safe to test out and polish your approach. You want to learn from those that know more than you, but you also want to leave a positive impression with those you meet and gain insight into the best ways to proceed in your job search.

The process used in these types of interviews will serve not just the job-searching candidates that use it but be a valuable tool in conducting market research and in building a lifelong network of contacts.

As with most things in life, the investment you put in will yield more fruitful results. So, if the job search process gets frustrating, may this resource can be your guiding light to put yourself out there. Asking the right questions will lead to the answers you need to get ahead, and earn the job you want.

In Conclusion, the Power of Gratitude

All the inspiration and motivation in the world can't stop negative emotions like doubt and insecurity to creep in from time to time. You may feel overwhelmed at times, perhaps even hopeless.

But there is an emotion we can choose to have and embrace in order to balance the darkness out. "Gratitude is an emotion that grounds us and is a great way to balance out the negative mindset that uncertainty engenders," said Dr. Guy Winch, author of the book "Emotional First Aid."

The future undoubtedly holds uncertainty, and

oftentimes, that uncertainty can instill fear in us, seizing us into inaction.

The process of choosing to feel grateful compels us to reflect on our relationships, leading us to feel closer and more connected to others. This helps motivate and sustain our efforts at self-improvement. When we're motivated by negative emotions, such as bitterness, resentment or revenge, it is nearly impossible to sustain efforts to change in a positive way. We will fail to find happiness if the motivation is achieved through negative means.

Therefore, gratitude precedes happiness.

Gratitude results in being willing and ready to show appreciation and return kindness. It brings a warm feeling of thankfulness towards the world, or towards specific individuals.

Gratitude helps people feel more positive emotions, feel more alive, express more compassion, relish good experiences, improve their health, deal with adversity and build strong relationships.

With gratitude, you will be inspired to serve others, like one day grant others informational interviews about your industry, just as others had done for you. Happiness is found when your service is performed not expecting something in return, and if your intention is to help and lessen other people's misery.

So, if you're miserable in your job, feeling stuck in life, stressed over what your future holds, don't be surprised when you finally discover your calling after focusing on helping others rather than yourself.

With gratitude, and this perspective, you will find that you're not alone. Everyone needs help sometimes, and help is available to you too if you're strong enough to ask for it.

Your personal development takes one step and one day at a time, but by being actively curious about yourself, others, while keeping a perspective of gratitude, that murky job search or journey toward happiness will become clearer before your eyes, like a dark cloud making way for the bright sunshine.

Connected Events Matter: Website

https://connectedeventsmatter.com/

Brent Jones is the creator of Connected Events Matter and a long-time career coach who knows the importance of personal development and being able to reinvent yourself throughout your life. Brent has been through all of this, and he loves helping others realize that change can be tremendous when the right choices are made.

The website brings together Brent's life experience to put you on the path to happiness and success. As our lives change, so too does our perspective, and we start to see events in our past and present through a different lens. Learn how this new perception changes us and how our choices at each stage of our lives make us who we are.

The website includes sections on the authors books, favorite authors and books, reviews, poetry, and over 20 sections on life development.

Reinventing Ourselves is a consistent theme in the website sections. Brent's passion is about trying to be better each day and to find new ideas that will help us to do that.

Thank you for reading!

The Human Factor:

How Finding Your Dream Job Starts By
Getting To Know Yourself

Amazon Reviews

Please remember to write a review of this book
on my Amazon Author page:
amazon.com/author/brentjones

Amazon Author Page

To order further books or view additional titles, visit
Amazon Author Page: https://www.amazon.com/Brent---
M.-Jones/e/B07WTRSLC1

Other Books by Brent M. Jones

Work Matters: Insights and Strategies for Job Seekers in a Rapidly Changing Economy

A job for most of us is more than just the way we make a living. It shapes how we see ourselves, as well as how others see us. It gives our days structure, purpose, and meaning. But in a rapidly changing marketplace — reshaped in recent years by technology and automation and devastated in 2020 by a global pandemic that has left millions out of work — finding a job has become exponentially more challenging. In Work Matters, author and career development coach Brent M. Jones reflects on the current environment and what the implications are for those seeking work and offers insights on how to navigate the disruption with proven, time-tested job-search strategies.

Embrace Life's Randomness: Breathe in the Amazing

Our journeys through life follow unexpected paths. Sometimes, looking back offers clarity and understanding, while other times you find yourself at an unforeseen junction and it takes your breath away. When the unexpected happens, it can be wonderful, challenging or both, yet the way you approach such events is key to your spiritual happiness and growth. In Embrace Life's Randomness, author Brent M. Jones considers whether the unexpected is truly random and compares the traditional stoic determinist view of life with a view more accepting of randomness and free will.

Why Life Stories Change: As You Look at Your Own Life Story, You See Yourself Differently

We have a choice in putting together the narrative of who we are, and who we become. We can pick which of the events we connect with, what we conclude about them, and then weave and reweave them into our story. As my story changes with the retelling, I find that it changes me. I become different because of how I see the story. In Why Life Stories Change, author Brent M. Jones offers some thoughtful reflections on how the events of our lives can be reshaped over time, resulting in positive changes in our self-identity.

Networking With a Purpose: The Informational Interview

Ever hear anyone say this during a frustrating job search? "They got the job because they knew somebody." "They were hired because of their connections." By following this simple guide to build your professional network, you can be that person who has that coveted edge over the competition.

The Interview of Self: How Looking Inside Can Help You Find Happiness and Success

There is a distinction between broken people and those looking to improve; give meaning to your own live and inspire for reach for something more.

sustainably continue making small inner and outer upgrades for your own personal development by becoming more self-aware of your identity. You need a change, and in order to get that, you need to change.

Make The First Step Towards Your New YOU!

Author's Biography

Brent M. Jones is a career development coach, consultant, author, and past Senior Business Executive. For years, Brent has been dedicated to motivating and educating people. He has helped hundreds of candidates to reevaluate themselves for a career change and acquire the skills needed for the job they desire while learning to navigate the marketplace. True to the words "Practice what you Preach", Brent established his very own entrepreneurial sales company that covered 15 Western states and helped hundreds of entrepreneurs grow their businesses. Besides, he has helped multiple large companies with business operations and during the process, developed a new perspective of the business world.

Brent reinvented himself while assisting people in finding new jobs and realized the importance of networking and relationships in their true sense. Brent doesn't only give directions but truly feels it in his heart to make a difference in peoples' lives. His books and blogs are clear proof of how deeply he connects to people's emotional aspects.

He has carefully curated detailed and real-life insights on succeeding in job seeking with actionable advice.

Brent believes in adapting to the changes with innovative strategies that will help people follow their passion and attain success while inspiring them to listen to their inner voices.

\

Made in the USA
Coppell, TX
02 January 2025

43775300R10046